THE WHISPERING KNIGHTS

When William, Susie, and Martha cook a witch's brew in the old barn, they don't really expect anything to happen. Witches are just superstition, William says. Nobody believes in them today.

But there are stories in the village that the barn was once a witch's home. And then the children see old Miss Hepplewhite standing in the doorway. She tells them that there *is* a witch. Her name is Morgan le Fay, and she comes from a much older time, when knights rode into battle on horseback, and everybody believed in witches. 'There has been no sign of her for many, many years,' Miss Hepplewhite says. 'But she's always here somewhere. She's the bad side of things, you see.'

A cool wind has begun to blow, and in the shadowy places in the barn there are strange little noises. The three children, even calm, sensible Susie, suddenly feel very cold, icy cold . . .

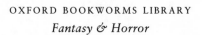

OXFORD BOOKWORMS LIBRARY
Fantasy & Horror

The Whispering Knights

Stage 4 (1400 headwords)

Series Editor: Jennifer Bassett
Founder Editor: Tricia Hedge
Activities Editors: Jennifer Bassett and Alison Baxter

PENELOPE LIVELY

The
Whispering Knights

Retold by
Clare West

Illustrated by
Toby Carr

OXFORD UNIVERSITY PRESS
2000

Oxford University Press,
Great Clarendon Street, Oxford OX2 6DP

Oxford New York
Athens Auckland Bangkok Bogotá Buenos Aires Calcutta Cape Town
Chennai Dar es Salaam Delhi Florence Hong Kong Istanbul Karachi
Kuala Lumpur Madrid Melbourne Mexico City Mumbai Nairobi
Paris São Paulo Singapore Taipei Tokyo Toronto Warsaw
and associated companies in
Berlin Ibadan

OXFORD and OXFORD ENGLISH
are trade marks of Oxford University Press

ISBN 0 19 423054 6

Original edition © Penelope Lively 1971
First published by William Heinemann Ltd 1971
This simplified edition © Oxford University Press 2000

First published in Oxford Bookworms 1996
This second edition published in the Oxford Bookworms Library 2000

Typeset by Wyvern Typesetting Ltd, Bristol
Printed in Spain by Unigraf s.l.

CONTENTS

1
The witch's brew

The frogs' legs weren't as bad as the children had expected. They slid quickly out of the tin and into the pan, which Susie was holding over the fire. Although they were greyish-brown and very unpleasant, Martha was relieved to see that they didn't look like real legs. She had been feeling sorry for the poor frogs.

But William was looking crossly into the pan. 'We paid a lot for them!' he said. 'I hope they're worth it.'

The children had made a small fire just inside the door of the barn. They often came to play here, as it was only just outside the village of Steeple Hampden, where they

'I hope they're worth it.'

1

lived. Nobody else seemed to use the big, empty building. The barn's old walls were made of rough stone, which appeared to change colour when the sunlight touched it, and the barn roof had green and gold plants climbing all over it. On the other side of the building was a big house, standing alone in the middle of the fields. Inside the barn, the only light came through the large double doors and one or two holes in the roof. So it was difficult to see into all the corners, which always looked dark and mysterious.

It was William who had first suggested making a witch's brew, some weeks before. He had got the idea from his father, who was a teacher at the village school.

'It's what witches used to do!' he had told Susie and Martha excitedly. 'You know, put all kinds of things into a pan, and heat it over a fire. We can collect all the things, and make a fire in the barn. It'll be fun! Just a small fire, of course. We won't be able to play there any more if we cause any damage. Look, I've written it all down. My dad told me what we need. It's in an old book he's got. Look – here's the list!'

With eye of fish, and toe of frog,
Wool of sheep, and hair of dog,
Oil of rose, and skin of snake,
And wing of bird, the brew make.

'How can we find all these things?' Susie had asked. Her eyes were bright with interest.

'It's easy!' said William delightedly. 'We can buy a bottle of rose oil, a tin of those little fish with their heads on for

2

the eye of fish and . . .'

'Toe of frog! How do we manage that?' asked Susie.

'No problem,' replied William. 'You can get frogs' legs in tins. People eat them.'

The girls stared at him in horror.

'Honestly, it's true. We can order a tin from a shop in London. And we can find a dead bird in the woods. *And* a snake skin, if we look carefully. And . . .'

But Martha was feeling very worried. 'Do you think this is a good idea?' she asked. 'I mean, it sounds like a spell to me. Is it really safe?'

'It's not a *spell*,' William answered, 'it's like science. We're going to see what happens. It'll be very interesting!'

'But –' Martha went on unhappily, 'when you listen to all the stories in the village about the witch who used to live in the barn, couldn't it be – er – dangerous?'

'You don't really believe all that rubbish, do you?' said William. 'Witches and all that? That was just superstition – what people in the past used to believe. You see, they wanted someone to blame when they were ill or their cows died or something. So they said there were witches who put spells on things. But there aren't any! That's what my dad says, and he knows.'

Martha was still very doubtful, but she had to agree to the plan, because the three of them always did things together. In the next couple of weeks they busily collected what they needed for the witch's brew, as well as some firewood.

Now here they were, on a Tuesday morning in August, all staring at a pan full of strange things on a very small fire. Susie, who was doing the cooking, had already said the words of the old song that William had copied from his father's book.

Wind blow, and night bird sing,
Fire burn, and trouble bring.

After a while she said crossly, 'This fire's no good! The brew's never going to get hot!'

William and Martha looked into the pan. The frogs' legs no longer looked like anything at all, but the bird's wing was still recognizable.

Martha looked away quickly. 'What's going to happen?' she whispered in a frightened little voice.

'Nothing,' said Susie. *She* wasn't afraid. But then nothing ever frightened her. She was only a few months older than Martha, but she seemed years older and was much more confident. 'I'd like to be more like Susie,' thought Martha, looking at her friend's round, sensible face. William wasn't afraid either. 'But it was his idea,' thought Martha, 'and anyway he's cleverer than Susie or me.' The square of yellow sunlight falling on to the stone floor from the open door suddenly disappeared, and Martha felt cold.

'What do we do with this, anyway?' said Susie, staring at the unpleasant greyish soup in the pan. 'What did witches do with it when they'd made it?' She looked accusingly at William.

'I – er, I don't know,' said William. He had wanted to

4

make a witch's brew in the place where people said a witch had once lived. But now they had actually made it, he couldn't remember at all what he had planned to do with it. He looked disappointedly at the brew. 'Throw it away, I suppose,' he said.

'Or eat it, perhaps,' said Susie, with a quick look at Martha, who felt suddenly sick. Now that the sun had gone, it was cold and dark in the barn, and the brew was beginning to smell bad as it got warmer. A little wind blew across the stone floor and made strange sad noises in the roof. The children went on staring at the pan.

At first they did not notice that a fourth person had joined them. She stood watching them for several minutes before any of them saw her.

At last she spoke. 'A witch's brew, is it?'

They all jumped. Martha saw only her black shape against the light in the doorway, but saw that she was old and bent, with a stick. Martha gave a little scream, and put her hands over her face, her whole body shaking.

'A witch's brew, is it?'

5

William, who was closer, saw the person more clearly. He realized she must be the old lady who lived in the house next to the barn. Miss Hepplewhite, wasn't that her name? He hoped that she would not stop them playing in the barn.

Susie was the one who answered. 'Yes, it is,' she said.

Miss Hepplewhite stepped into the barn. 'Ah,' she said, touching the empty tin of frogs' legs with the end of her stick, 'very clever! And how did you find the other things?'

They told her, and she listened carefully. From the expression on her face, it was impossible to see what she was thinking.

At last Martha asked, trembling, 'Does it matter? Have we done anything wrong?'

The fire was no longer burning, and the brew was getting cold. Outside, the wind had stopped, and into the dark stillness came heavy drops of rain, like fingers touching the leaves of trees.

'I don't know that you have done anything wrong,' replied Miss Hepplewhite. 'But it is possible that you have done something rather dangerous.'

They all looked up at her, surprised. Martha's stomach turned. 'I knew it wasn't safe!' she thought. 'But they wouldn't listen to me!'

William said, 'But witches with tall hats and black cats and so on, that's just superstition. There wasn't ever a witch here.'

'Not a witch like that, I agree,' said Miss Hepplewhite.

'But there was *something* here. *She* was here for a time, you see.'

'She?' said William. 'Who is she?'

'Don't you children know about her? She is Morgan le Fay, who was King Arthur's sister, hundreds of years ago. She is also the Ice Queen, and many others. She has appeared in many different shapes, and with many different names, but in the end I always recognize her. She comes from a time much

'She had – has – places everywhere.'

older than ours, but she's always here somewhere. She does all she can to destroy what is good – she's the bad side of things, you see.'

The children were very quiet.

'What do you mean – she was here for a time?' asked William.

'This barn was one of her places. She had – has – places everywhere. While people believe that there *are* witches, she stays, but as soon as people begin to forget about her, and laugh when someone says there's a witch in the barn, then it's time for her to go somewhere else. That's what happened here.'

7

'So she's gone right away from here,' Susie said, looking relieved.

Miss Hepplewhite said nothing, and stared at the remains of the fire.

'*Has* she gone?' asked William, watching Miss Hepplewhite.

'I thought so,' said Miss Hepplewhite at last. 'There has been no sign of her for many, many years. But I know she watches the places that have once been hers, like this barn. And if she finds people who still believe . . .'

In the corners of the barn, and in the shadowy places in the roof, the children could hear strange little noises. 'It's nothing,' Martha told herself. 'The barn's always like this, it talks to itself.'

Miss Hepplewhite moved towards the door. It had stopped raining outside, but the sky was heavy, with grey clouds on the hills.

'Luckily,' she continued, 'she was always less interested in children.'

'How will we know if she's interested in us?' asked Martha.

'Oh, you'll know all right. If she has noticed you, she'll look for your weaknesses. You'll have to be careful. And now I must go.' She turned and walked quickly away towards a door in the wall surrounding her house. Although she did not say goodbye, or look back at them, the children had a strong feeling that she expected to see them again.

Martha watched her go, and suddenly realized how cold she felt. Her whole body felt like ice. She could not remember ever feeling so cold before. And when she looked at Susie, who had plenty of fat to keep her warm, she saw that her friend was trembling with cold too.

Just then William said, 'I'm frozen! Strange, isn't it?'

'It's the rain,' said Susie. 'That's made us feel cold. Time to go home.'

'That's it,' agreed William. 'It's the rain.'

'Oh, do you think so?' said Martha, in a relieved voice.

'Oh yes,' said William confidently. 'Come on, let's go home now.'

Once they were outside, they began to feel warmer as they ran back to Steeple Hampden together, in the thin evening sunshine.

2
Morgan appears

Later that evening, while having supper with her family, Martha told them that she had met Miss Hepplewhite. She did not mention anything else that had happened at the barn.

'Is she still alive, and living up there in the big house?' asked her father in surprise. 'I remember her when I was a boy, and she wasn't young then. You'd better be polite to her, if you want to go on playing in that barn.

It belongs to her, you know.'

'Does it?' said Martha. The children were used to hearing the villagers tell them to go away, or make less noise. She felt grateful to Miss Hepplewhite, who hadn't said anything like that.

Mrs Timms was helping Martha's two little brothers to eat their supper, but now she looked up. 'I don't think you should spend so much time in that barn, Martha. We don't know what you're doing there, do we? And it's cold there, with those old stone floors. You're only wearing a thin dress.'

'No, really, Mum, it isn't cold,' replied Martha. 'And William's there too,' she added, rather cleverly for her.

'Ah,' said her mother, sounding a little relieved. 'That William's a sensible boy.'

'The teacher's son?' said Mr Timms, finishing his last piece of bread. 'Yes, a very nice boy. Very polite.'

'I'm surprised that he's still got time for you and Susie,' said her mother. 'Boys of his age usually like to be with other *boys*, not girls.'

Martha said, 'He doesn't like what the other boys do – just fighting, that kind of thing. He likes doing things with us.'

'For example?' asked her father, lighting his pipe and sitting back in his armchair. He looked all ready for a long, comfortable conversation.

'Oh, just things,' said Martha quickly. She knew that she was no good at keeping secrets, and had to escape before her parents discovered any more from her. 'I think I'll have my bath now, Mum,' she said, and hurried upstairs.

She could not forget what had happened that afternoon, although she was trying very hard to think of something else. What would happen now, because of the witch's brew? Would the witch called Morgan appear? These questions worried Martha all evening. 'And I'm sure I'll dream about all this tonight, and wake up crying as usual!' she thought.

She often used to sleep badly. Her dreams were full of faceless ghosts, mysterious dark figures and other nameless horrors, chasing her as she tried to escape. She always woke up crying, in great fear. It took her some time to calm down and realize that she was safe at home in her own bed.

William and Susie did not have this problem. William only dreamed of exciting adventures. 'And I'm always the captain or the leader in the dream!' he said. 'Fantastic!' Susie said that she never dreamed, 'unless I've eaten too much!'

When Martha woke up in the middle of the night, she felt cold. 'But I *haven't* been dreaming!' she thought. 'Perhaps I've been woken by a storm, although everything's quiet now.' She was just going to turn over and go to sleep again, when she noticed something on the far side of the room. There was a shadow on the floor, and she had the feeling that just before she looked at it, it had moved.

Now the shadow was half on the floor and half on the wall, and looked like an old, bent woman dressed in black, with her head covered.

'It's a shadow made by the curtain,' thought Martha, and quickly pulled back the curtain at the window above her bed. But the shadow did not move. Martha pulled the blankets round herself, her heart beating loudly and her body shaking.

She will look for your weaknesses . . .

'Well, she won't find them,' Martha told herself suddenly. 'Shadows on the wall, in the darkness! I *used* to be afraid of that kind of thing, but not any more. Morgan won't succeed that way!' And very quickly, while she still felt brave enough, she jumped out of bed and ran to the door, to turn on the electric light. The room was immediately filled with bright yellow light. The shadow stayed for a second or two, and then disappeared.

Martha got back into bed. To her surprise, she did not really feel frightened. 'Morgan was here,' she thought. 'I'm

But the shadow did not move.

almost certain she was. But I didn't give in!' With the light still on, she lay down and went to sleep again.

The next morning, as they were walking to the barn, she told William and Susie what had happened to her in the night.

Susie laughed. 'You're stupid, Martha, you are. It was just a bad dream, that's all.'

'It wasn't,' said Martha. 'This was different.'

'How long did the shadow stay after you turned the light on?' asked William. 'One second? Two?'

'I didn't actually count,' said Martha. 'But it was long enough for me to be sure that it wasn't just a shadow.'

The barn lay ahead of them, its roof gold in the sunshine. Inside, everything was normal. It was cool and quiet.

Susie noticed a big pile of straw in the corner. 'We could put some straw on the floor to sit on,' she suggested, and went over to pick some up. Suddenly she jumped backwards with a scream.

'What's the matter?' asked William.

'Something moved under there!' cried Susie, who was usually the calmest of people.

'Probably a cat,' said William.

'No. Bigger than that. You can get the straw yourself. I'm not going near it again.'

William walked across the floor and looked at the thick, dusty pile of straw. He touched it with his foot, and the whole of one end moved. They all three ran to the door.

'There really *is* something there,' said William.

'*Now* do you believe me?' said Martha, pleased. 'About what happened to me in the night?'

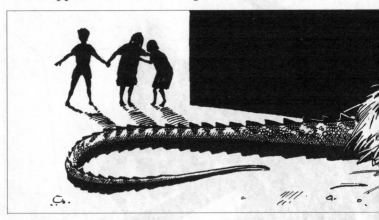

They stood frozen with fear in the doorway.

14

'This could be quite different,' said Susie crossly.

They stood in the doorway, watching the straw, and ready to run at any moment. Nothing happened. William picked up a stone and threw it at the straw. And then, very slowly, the straw moved again. They stared in horror, as something began to come out of one end of the pile, making an unpleasant noise as it slid like a snake over the stone floor. It was a tail – dark, thick and round, with a smooth, shiny skin, and it had a large foot, with claws. They could see the shape of an ugly black head under the straw.

The children could not move. They stood frozen with fear in the doorway. And then suddenly William said, 'Look! Look at its head! See what it's doing!'

Smoke was rising from the straw, and as they watched, flames appeared, and the straw began to burn.

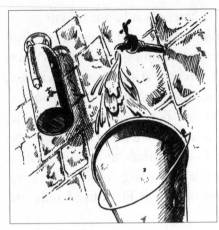

'Water! Quick!'

'Water!' shouted William. 'Quick! There's a tap and an old bucket outside!'

The whole of the pile was now on fire, and the thing's shiny tail was beating happily on the floor, as the children threw water on the straw. There was a hissing sound, but the flames went on burning. William ran outside and pulled the old fire extinguisher off the wall. 'It probably won't work, it's so old!' he thought. But when he banged it on the ground, thick white foam came out, and he managed to point the heavy extinguisher at the straw. Clouds of black smoke filled the barn, and the white foam went all over the straw and the floor. There was a terrible smell, and a loud hissing noise. The children ran outside, almost unable to breathe.

Little by little, the smoke disappeared, and they looked fearfully back into the barn. The pile of straw was blackened and burnt, but there was nothing else there.

'There!' said Martha. 'Just like last night, but this time we all saw it, not just me. You were *brave*, William.'

'Actually I didn't really stop to think,' he said.

16

'We ought to tell Miss Hepplewhite,' said Martha.

Susie, whose normally pink face was white, looked doubtful. 'Do you really think she'll believe us if we tell her we've seen a big shiny thing with claws, which breathed smoke, and started a fire, and then just disappeared?'

'Yes,' said Martha simply.

So they went to the door in the wall that led into Miss Hepplewhite's garden. They had never opened that door before, but they all felt that yesterday there had been an unspoken invitation. They entered a big garden, which had once been well cared for, but was now rather untidy. Miss Hepplewhite was cutting roses and putting them into a shallow basket. She was wearing a very large old summer hat.

'Excuse me,' said William politely, 'but I'm afraid we have to tell you something.'

'Well,' said Miss Hepplewhite, looking up from her flowers, 'I suppose that Morgan has come?'

They looked at each other, all rather reluctant to tell the story. At last William spoke, with Martha adding her bit about the shadow in the night.

'I'm sorry about the foam and the burnt straw in the barn,' William said at the end.

'Oh, don't worry about that,' said Miss Hepplewhite carelessly. 'Come and sit down for a moment.' They all sat down in chairs in front of the large old stone house. 'I must say, I don't think much of her first attempt. You're far too intelligent to be frightened by that.' She smiled at

17

them, and Martha felt warm inside. Somehow Miss Hepplewhite's good opinion seemed very important.

'Was it all right about the fire extinguisher?' asked William worriedly.

'An excellent idea. Always try to surprise her. Never play the game her way. We have to fight against her with reason, and science. She knows very little about either of them.'

'Do you think she'll come back?' asked Susie.

Miss Hepplewhite thought for a moment. 'Probably,' she replied at last. 'But you've made a good start. Perhaps *we* should take the next step now, while we have the advantage over her. It could help us to win the fight against her.'

'How?' asked William, interested.

'Well, we could have a Walpurgis Night. Do you know about that? I can see that you don't. It was done in villages in the old days, to drive out witches. People used to march through the streets making as much noise as possible. We'd have to do it round the barn. This evening would be best. Do you think your parents would agree to that?'

The children looked at each other doubtfully.

'Perhaps if I write to your parents personally,' suggested Miss Hepplewhite cleverly, 'inviting you all to take tea with me? We will not mention anything to do with the Walpurgis idea.'

They all agreed that this would probably work. So Miss Hepplewhite wrote each of them a polite invitation, on

They began to enjoy this new experience.

thick, expensive writing-paper, in very black ink, for their parents.

The plan was successful, and just after dark that evening all three of them arrived back at the barn. Miss Hepplewhite was already there, surrounded by a large number of hand bells, metal plates and spoons, pots, pans, and an old gun.

'Help yourselves!' she cried. 'Make as much noise as you can!' At first it was difficult for the children. They couldn't remember anyone ever *telling* them to make a noise before. But soon they began to enjoy this new experience. They ran enthusiastically up and down outside the barn, banging the pots and pans with the spoons, ringing the bells, and shouting and screaming loudly. Miss Hepplewhite watched them, looking very pleased. She was burning some green plants in front of the barn, so there was a strong, rather strange smell in the air. At last the children all fell on the ground, exhausted.

'Excellent!' said Miss Hepplewhite. 'Morgan will not like that at all!'

'Do you think we've sent her away?' asked William.

Miss Hepplewhite looked round. It was suddenly silent, after all the noise, and darkness covered everything. In the trees a bird gave a warning cry, and then was quiet. 'We shall have to wait and see,' she said. 'Now what about something to eat? Your tea is ready in the house.'

3
A cake for Susie

The days passed, and things were peaceful up at the barn. At first the children were very careful, and looked closely at every shadow, and every dark corner. But nothing happened.

'I think Morgan's gone. She was frightened of us,' said Susie confidently one day.

Martha was not so sure. She said nothing.

'You know something?' said William. 'We ought to ask Miss Hepplewhite to tea. It'd be polite – to say thank you for inviting *us* to tea. And anyway, she's nice.'

Susie considered. 'Where would it be?'

'Here. In the barn,' answered William. 'I know it belongs to her, but she'll understand.'

Susie looked doubtful, but Martha said at once, 'Oh yes! We can tidy up the barn, and put some flowers on an old box for a table, and bring food from home.'

'I suppose I could bring some food from Mum's shop,' said Susie reluctantly. 'She probably wouldn't notice.'

So the tea-party was arranged. Miss Hepplewhite arrived, wearing a long dress made of a beautiful material that whispered as she walked, lots of rings on her bony fingers, and a very large summer hat which was covered in flowers. The food was certainly different from Miss Hepplewhite's tea. Instead of her thin sandwiches, light sugared cakes, and tea from a silver pot, they had cold chicken, pieces of cheese, chocolate, apples, and bottles of fruit drinks. Miss Hepplewhite enjoyed it all, and thanked them most politely when she finally left. The children felt that the tea-party had been a great success.

Later that afternoon Susie was helping her mother in the village shop when one of the customers began talking about the plans for the new motorway several kilometres away from the village. Susie's mother was proud of knowing everything that happened in and around the village. 'You know, Mrs Slater,' she said, filling a paper bag with apples, 'at one time that motorway was going to come right through the Sharnbrook valley here.'

'Never! That'd destroy half the village. What a terrible thing, Mrs Poulter!' replied Mrs Slater.

'Then, luckily, they decided to build it on the far side of Chipping Ledbury, where that big factory is. People say that Mr Steel, who owns the factory, will get a lot of money for pulling his factory down so that the motorway can be

21

built. He's rich enough already, that's what I say! That comes to one pound fifty, please, Mrs Slater.'

'Here you are. Well, it's a good thing for us, anyway. A motorway through the village! I hope I never live to see it.'

Susie listened without much interest, and when it was time to close the shop, went through to the sitting-room. She turned on the television, but the only picture that appeared was an unending shower of white rain. She decided to go round to Martha's house to watch television, and went out of the back door. But as she passed the front of the shop, she noticed something on the doorstep. It was a large parcel, addressed to Miss Susie Poulter, with 'By Hand' written in one corner.

She sat down on the step, and opened the parcel. Inside, there was a white box, and inside *that*, there was a cake. A large, round cake, beautifully made. She had never seen anything like it. On its perfect top, in smooth pink and white writing, it said 'To dear Susie, with love'.

'It's not my birthday,' thought Susie, thinking hard. 'Who could it possibly be from?' There was no card or letter in the box. Could it be

It was a large parcel.

from her mother? No, the cake was clearly a very expensive one, and Mrs Poulter was careful with money. From her aunt? But Aunt Pam lived far away in Nottingham. How could she get a cake here by hand? It was a real mystery.

Susie decided not to tell her mother about it. It would be more fun to take it to the barn, and give some to William and Martha. After all, it said 'To dear Susie' on it, so it was *her* cake, and she could do what she liked with it. She put it back in the box, and took it round to Martha's house to show her.

She found Martha sitting on the gate outside her house.

'I want to watch your television,' said Susie. 'There's something wrong with ours.'

'Is there?' Martha replied. 'Ours isn't working either.'

'Let's see,' said Susie, who believed nobody. They went into the Timms' kitchen and turned on the television. The same shower of white rain appeared.

'It's pretty,' said Martha, staring dreamily at it.

'Don't be stupid!' answered Susie crossly. 'Come on, then, let's go out.' They went outside, and she took the parcel from under her arm. 'Here, I've got something to show you.' She opened the cake-box.

'Oh, Susie!' cried Martha, her eyes widening in surprise. 'You are *lucky*, Susie! Who sent it to you?'

'I don't know,' replied Susie. 'There was no card or anything. I thought we could eat it at the barn tomorrow.'

'Oh yes!' said Martha delightedly.

Susie looked lovingly at the cake. 'It wouldn't matter if

we tasted a bit now, would it?' she suggested.

So Martha ran to the kitchen for a knife, and Susie cut two thin pieces very carefully out of the beautiful cake. She passed the first one to Martha on the side of her knife, but her hand shook a little and the piece of cake fell on the grass. 'Sorry,' she said. Martha picked it up and opened her mouth to take a bite, when Susie said suddenly, 'Stop a minute. Look there!'

Martha looked, still holding the piece of cake in her hand. Where the cake had been on the ground, the grass was brown and burnt. Martha gasped, and dropped her piece of cake. The skin on her fingers was pink, and felt painful.

'Susie – there's something wrong with it!'

Susie bent over the cake, and smelt it. It did not smell of sugar or butter or fruit, but of something bad. She jumped up, found a stick lying in the grass, and pushed it down hard, right into the centre of the cake. There was a hissing noise and a terribly bad smell, and then, where the cake had been, nothing but a circle of burnt grass.

The girls stared in horror.

There was a hissing noise.

24

'We nearly ate it!' said Susie. 'Think what your stomach would be like if you ate that!'

A freezing cold entered their bones, and their arms and legs felt strangely heavy. The sky seemed to become darker, and there was a feeling of danger in the air. Martha and Susie looked at each other uncomfortably. 'It was Morgan, wasn't it?' whispered Susie, and Martha whispered back, 'Yes.' The smell was still very strong. Without another word they hurried away and ran into Martha's house.

'What's wrong with you two?' asked Mrs Timms. 'You look very white. Have you seen a ghost?'

Martha was still shaking, but Susie was beginning to feel better. 'It's raining,' she said, 'that's all.'

The next day they told Miss Hepplewhite about the cake. She just laughed. 'Oh really, I am afraid that Morgan will have to do better than that! How childish of her! She does not realize how sensible you are. We shall have no problems if she continues like this.'

Susie and Martha were rather ashamed that they had come so near to eating the cake. But Miss Hepplewhite was much more interested in the problems that they were all having with their televisions.

'All our televisions have gone wrong in the same way,' explained William, 'and it only happens when *we're* in the room! Do you think it could be . . .'

Miss Hepplewhite thought for a moment. 'How do they work, these machines?' she asked.

'Well,' said William importantly, 'it's all a question of

sound waves, you see. They . . . er . . . go through the air, and . . . well, I'm not certain how they *do* work, actually.'

'If it *is* anything to do with her, then it is worrying,' said Miss Hepplewhite, 'because it means she is moving on to our ground, and into our time. I wonder . . . Morgan knows very little about new ideas. She may think television is more central to our lives than it really is.'

'I'm sorry,' said Susie. 'I don't really understand.'

'Well, consider the evenings in your home, and millions of other homes. The circle of chairs all turned to face the television, the polite silence broken only by the confident voice from the box . . .'

'Oh!' said William. 'I see! She thinks it's a kind of god!'

'It is possible that Morgan has made that mistake. So we do not need to worry too much about this latest attempt of hers to frighten you.'

The next day it rained heavily all morning, and Susie decided to stay and help her mother in the shop, as it was too wet to go to the barn. For a while, things were quiet.

Then at ten o'clock Mrs Watts came in. 'Well, what a day! It's black Friday for us all right, isn't it?'

Susie's mother looked at the window. 'What else can you expect? Seems to me it always rains a lot in August.'

'I'm not talking about the weather!' said Mrs Watts impatiently. 'I mean the other business. Haven't you heard?'

Mrs Poulter hated not knowing the latest news. She had to pretend she wasn't very interested. 'Other business?'

'All because that awful old man's decided something

26

different now. He's got friends in the right places, that's what people say. Well, I think Tom and I'll just have to move away.'

Mrs Poulter couldn't stop herself asking, 'What's the matter, then?'

'The matter! It's the motorway, that's what it is! They've changed the way it's going to go. It won't go south, past Chipping Ledbury, where the factory is. It'll go north through the valley, after all.'

Mrs Poulter stared. 'Will it be near the village, then?'

'Near! It'll go straight through it!'

4
The Hampden Stones

Soon everybody in the village was talking worriedly about the new motorway. Mrs Poulter had a wonderful time, collecting information as people flowed in and out of her shop.

'Lots of houses will be pulled down, you'll see.'

'We'll be shaken to pieces by the traffic!'

'The road will go through the farm, so that means my husband'll lose his job, if the land and the cows are sold.'

'There'll be noise, and dirt, and nothing but trouble!'

'I've lived here all my life. I don't want them to destroy my home to make way for a road!'

Susie, who had been listening carefully, suddenly asked,

'Why have the plans changed? I thought the road was going through Mr Steel's factory, near Chipping Ledbury?'

'Seems he suddenly decided he didn't want to lose his factory after all,' said one of the customers. 'So he contacted all his important friends, and they managed to get the plans changed. Now it'll go straight through Steeple Hampden.'

'It's a terrible thing,' said Mrs Poulter. 'A lovely valley like this, and a beautiful village.'

'People say it's all his wife's fault,' said someone darkly. 'Mr Steel's old now, but he's got a new young wife, and it seems she's persuaded him to do this.'

Susie reported all this to William and Martha. 'The road'll go through our barn, Mum says,' she told them unhappily. 'Then where'll we play?'

William had never felt so angry before. 'It's not right!' he said, his face red. 'We can't just let them destroy our favourite places! There must be *something* we can do to stop it.'

That afternoon the children decided to go and tell Miss Hepplewhite about the motorway. The rain had stopped and the sun was shining as they walked slowly through the village. It was more beautiful, and more peaceful, than they had ever seen it. The old stone of the houses looked golden in the sunshine, and the gardens were full of sweet-smelling flowers. The children did not feel like talking as they crossed the field in front of the barn. They went straight into Miss Hepplewhite's garden through the door in the wall.

Miss Hepplewhite listened with interest to William, as he explained about the new road. 'You say this is a sudden change of plan?' she asked, her eyes bright.

'Yes. It's this awful person called Mr Steel.'

Martha said in a small voice, 'I think someone's put a spell on him or something. I think it's all to do with Morgan.'

'Clever child,' said Miss Hepplewhite. 'No doubt about it. It is a disaster, I'm afraid. She has done the unexpected, and moved right on to our ground. This time *she* has surprised *us*.'

Susie's eyes widened. 'I don't understand,' she said. 'I mean, why would Morgan want a road to go through *her* barn?'

'It will still be her place, whatever is there. A piece of road, if it is on her ground, could easily be an evil place – a place where accidents happen.'

'But what can we do to stop her?' asked William.

'Be very careful. Watch for the unexpected. Remember – most people only see what they expect to see. I think she will be here in person now, and that is always when she is at her most dangerous. You will have to decide what steps to take against her. I am too old to fight her, and she knows that.'

Martha thought, 'Perhaps she has fought Morgan before. This must be why she knows so much about Morgan.'

'Well, we brought her here, didn't we?' said Susie, almost

*'She hates the sign
of the cross.'*

crossly. 'By making that witch's brew in the barn. So we'll *have* to fight her, won't we?'

Martha said, 'What do we do if – if she comes?'

'You must be very brave,' said Miss Hepplewhite seriously. 'And you must find your own weapons. I may not be able to help you. Remember – she hates the sign of the cross, and she does not understand reason or science.'

They left Miss Hepplewhite and began to walk back to the village. Suddenly Martha said, 'Let's go up to the Stones.'

'Good idea,' said William. He no longer felt angry, but strangely excited. 'We're the only ones who know what's really happening!' he thought. Aloud, he said, 'Wouldn't it be fantastic if we, just the three of us, *could* win the fight against Morgan?'

'It won't be easy,' said Susie. 'She can put spells on people and things, so that nothing's what it seems to be.'

'We'll have to remember that all the time,' said William. 'We'll have to be really clever.' He turned to Martha. 'Are you all right?' he asked kindly. 'Not frightened or anything?'

'I don't like it,' said Martha, her voice shaking, 'because

I don't know what's going to happen next. Yes, I *am* frightened.'

'You mustn't be,' said Susie. 'Think of something else. Like what's for supper.'

They were climbing uphill now. The village of Steeple Hampden lay below them, with the River Sharnbrook running through the green valley. Further away were the roofs and chimneys of Chipping Ledbury. At the top of the hill they could see the grey shapes of the Hampden Stones, a circle of rough grey stones, half-buried deep in the grass, like old teeth. For thousands of years they had stood there, watching everything that happened in the valley. The villagers called them the Whispering Knights, and believed, or pretended to believe, that they were there to take care of the valley. Some people said that in times of trouble the Stones would leave their field and move. There was a story that in the old days the Stones had fought against an evil queen, and won. But for hundreds of years nobody had seen them move.

Ever since the children could remember, they had climbed on the Stones and played among them. It was one of Martha's favourite places, and she felt better as soon as she reached the stone circle. She stood on the tallest stone and stared out across the valley. 'We should see the road again soon,' she said. 'The corn's the right colour.'

They had first seen it last summer. It was William's father who had told them that, hidden somewhere in the cornfields, there could be an old, old road leading to the

A faint, darker line across the cornfield.

Stones. They had looked for it every day, in winter, summer, autumn and spring, but they had never seen anything. Until one day last summer, when the corn was high and golden-brown. And suddenly they had seen it, a faint, darker line across the cornfield, like a shadow. The next day, when the corn was cut, the line disappeared, and they had not seen it since.

They looked down at the village. 'Look at that big black car driving through!' said Martha suddenly. Nobody in Steeple Hampden owned a large, expensive car like that.

They hurried back down the hill and across the fields to the village, and saw the car, a big shiny black Rolls Royce, parked opposite Mrs Poulter's shop. In front sat a driver in uniform, and in the back there were two people.

'It must be that Mr Steel!' whispered Susie. 'He's the only rich man round here. And that'll be his new wife with him, I suppose.'

Just then the driver started the engine, and the car moved slowly down the road, towards the children. They stood by the church wall, as the car came closer. Now they could see the two people in the back of the car. One was a man in a dark suit. His hair was grey, and he looked rather old and tired.

Beside him was a woman, sitting with her long legs crossed. She was wearing an expensive-looking fur coat, and bright rings on her fingers. Her shining black hair lay smoothly against her head. And then, as the car passed the children, she turned and looked straight at them.

She turned and looked straight at them.

It was a long, cruel face, with a mouth that turned down at the corners. Her skin was bone-white and her hair shone like water. For long seconds she stared at them, and her eyes were terrible. They were black, and cold as ice, and evil.

The children could not move. They stood there, frozen, until the car had completely disappeared. Then at last William spoke. 'We'd better go and tell Miss Hepplewhite,' he said, 'that Morgan has actually been here, in Steeple Hampden.'

5
William's battle with Morgan

Miss Hepplewhite remained calm when they told her about Morgan. 'I expected this to happen,' she said.

'She looked normal at first,' said Martha. 'But when she looked at us, it was different. Then we *knew*.'

'Avoid looking at her,' said Miss Hepplewhite. 'She can persuade you to do something just by looking at you, if you are sensitive to that kind of thing.'

'What should we do next?' asked William.

'I have heard that your father is preparing a petition against the motorway. That is a very good idea. I suggest you should give him as much help as you can. It will annoy Morgan, and then perhaps she will start making mistakes.'

William's father was deeply involved in the fight against

the motorway. Their house was full of lists of names, maps, ringing telephones, and people coming and going. So the children offered to help. Their job was to visit as many villagers as possible, to explain where the new road would go, and what changes there would be to people's lives. It was not at all difficult to persuade them to sign the petition, as almost everybody was against the motorway.

'It's very successful so far,' said William's father proudly. 'I think *all* the local people are going to sign. *And* our story's in the Chipping Ledbury newspaper this week. I've talked to the reporter, and he agrees with us, so he's on our side! Perhaps that'll help persuade Mr Steel's friends that they're wrong!'

Susie said quietly to William, 'It's only a local paper. I don't suppose anyone in London reads it!'

But two days later something more exciting happened. For several seconds the village, with its green fields and old stone houses, appeared on television. Then the children, who were watching together, saw an interviewer, Mr Steel and the local newspaper reporter all sitting round a table.

'Now, Mr Steel,' said the interviewer politely, 'could you explain to us exactly why the motorway should go through the Sharnbrook valley, and not your factory at Chipping Ledbury?'

'Well,' said Mr Steel reluctantly, looking uncomfortable, 'I mean, people want motorways, don't they? Something has to go, doesn't it? Someone has to decide, you know!' All the time he was talking, he was looking rather wildly round the room, and he seemed to have difficulty in speaking clearly.

'You can see Morgan's put a spell on him,' said Susie, staring at him. 'He's behaving very strangely.'

When the local reporter was asked for *his* opinion, he became very excited, and waved his arms about. He talked enthusiastically of the 'unbelievably beautiful valley' and the 'fantastically attractive village'. But soon the interviewer was saying, 'Well, thank you, both of you. That's all we have time for tonight, I'm afraid! Good night!'

'We won,' said William, relieved. 'Easily. Anyone could see that. Mr Steel was hopeless.'

The villagers hoped that, now that the world had been shown the problem, something would happen. They waited. For a day or two the motorway story appeared in the national newspapers, and then it was forgotten. In the end they realized that people in the rest of the country were no longer interested in Steeple Hampden, and that they had not succeeded in changing anything. In a very short time, they would have to accept the unpleasant reality of a fast, wide road through the valley, destroying their homes, gardens, fields, and way of life.

'My Mum's always cross these days,' Susie told William and Martha one afternoon.

'I know. My Dad is, too,' answered William. 'They can't stop themselves. It's awful having to wait. You know something? I *hate* waiting. I wish something would happen.'

'Don't say that,' said Martha, looking frightened. 'Perhaps Morgan can hear you.'

'I don't care,' said William. They were passing the church, on their way up to the barn. He threw back his head and shouted, 'I WISH SOMETHING WOULD HAPPEN. I'M NOT AFRAID OF YOU.'

The children began to cross the field, and then, as they came closer, noticed that the big barn doors were wide open. Martha suddenly held on to Susie's arm. 'There's something in there!'

Out of the darkness came a figure. It stood in the doorway and looked out over the field. They could see the white of her face, the shine on her hair, and the fur coat over her shoulders. She was looking at them.

'Oh, William!' cried Martha. 'Why did you do that?'

'We'd better run while we can,' suggested Susie.

But William did not hear them. Seeing Morgan there, in *his* barn, made him very angry. Suddenly he started running as fast as he could across the grass, straight towards her. He felt big and strong and confident. 'I'm going to show her!' he thought. 'I'm going to make her go away!'

But the girls only saw a small, rather untidy figure running ahead of them. Susie shouted, 'Don't be stupid! What are you *doing*? Come back!' and Martha cried miserably, 'Oh Susie, whatever will happen to poor William?'

'*Now* we're in trouble,' said Susie crossly. 'Well, we

can't just leave him, can we?' And so both girls began to run across the field behind William.

He kept on running. All the time he could feel Morgan standing there, calm and silent, somewhere in front of him, waiting. And then he ran into her, shouting and hitting as hard as he could. Martha cried aloud. There was a wild hissing noise, and William was knocked backwards on the ground. Where Morgan had been standing, there was a large column of smooth stone, as tall as a woman.

William was knocked backwards on the ground.

38

Far away, in the clouds, there seemed to be a noise like a thin scream, and then the sky was silent again.

'What happened?' asked William, holding his head and getting up slowly. They all looked at the stone column. It was a rich green colour. When Martha touched it, it felt as cold as ice. She took her hand away quickly.

'Keep away from it,' said Susie. 'Remember the cake!'

Just then Miss Hepplewhite came through her garden door and walked towards them.

'It was her!' cried William. 'Morgan! She was here! And now there's – this – instead!'

'Ah,' said Miss Hepplewhite, looking at the column. 'Yes, the green stone – that's an old favourite of hers.'

'Will she come back?' asked Martha, in a low voice.

'Oh, no, she'll be far away by now. She had to escape, you see. She hates it if anyone touches or hits her. So that is an excellent way of fighting her. Clever of you, if I may say so,' she added, turning to William.

William was very pleased, and went red. 'I didn't plan it. I just got angry when I saw her at our barn. I mean, *your* barn.'

'Now the question is,' continued Miss Hepplewhite, 'what shall we do with this column? Could you possibly carry it into my garden? Then I think we'll make a hole through the middle, to give it a more interesting shape. Yes, that's it.'

With a lot of pushing and pulling, the children managed to move the heavy stone into Miss Hepplewhite's garden.

She brought out an electric drill. 'Here you are,' she said to William. 'I expect you know how to use this. Make a hole in the middle.'

William turned on the drill.

William turned on the drill. There was an unpleasant noise. And then, as the drill touched the stone, the whole thing disappeared. There was nothing left except a hole in the ground where the column had been.

'Oh dear,' said Miss Hepplewhite. 'How unfortunate!' But she did not sound at all surprised or disappointed. 'I think she knew what would happen!' thought Martha.

'We'd better go home now,' said Susie. She was angry with herself. Neither Martha nor William had allowed Morgan to find any weaknesses in them, but she, Susie, had very nearly eaten Morgan's cake.

But William could afford to be generous. 'Good thing Morgan saw you running up behind me,' he said carelessly.

'Do you really think that's what frightened her?'

'Oh yes,' said William. 'Yes, I'm sure that was it.'

6
Morgan and Martha

That night Martha dreamed. She dreamed of a milky-green sea, the colour of the stone column. It was calling her with soft, warm voices, but far away in another world, there was a thin voice screaming. She woke slowly, and somewhere outside her window there was a strange noise. Reluctantly she got out of bed and went to the window.

Outside it was unexpectedly bright. The moon, a perfect circle, hung above the hill, and clouds slid across its face like large grey fish. She could see the fields and trees, and could hear the wind beating at the walls of the houses. And somewhere right above it all, there was a high scream. Was it the wind? It was certainly nothing human or animal.

Martha knew she was hearing something that people are not supposed to hear, but at the same time she did not feel afraid. Although her hands and feet were cold, something made her stay at the window, away from her warm bed. The clouds disappeared, and everything was suddenly very bright. Now she could see grey shapes in the field. She knew what they were. It was difficult to see, but she thought that they were moving. The tops of the trees were blowing about wildly in the wind. And then, louder and nearer, came the scream, all around the house.

41

Martha's eyes opened very wide, like a cat's in the dark. Then she turned, and, moving like a machine, got back into bed and was asleep again in a few seconds.

When Susie arrived at the Timms' house after breakfast the next morning, she was surprised to find Martha sitting silently at the kitchen table, staring at her plate.

'Can Martha come and play?' she asked Mrs Timms.

'She doesn't seem very well,' replied Martha's mother.

'I'm all right,' said Martha, sounding cross. She did not look up or show any interest.

'Well, come on then,' said Susie. 'We're going to help William do some fishing, down at the river.'

Martha's two little brothers both started shouting, 'Can we go fishing too? Please can we go too?'

'You're too young,' said Mrs Timms. 'It isn't safe for you.'

Martha said nothing, but Susie felt sorry for the boys. 'I'll be responsible for them, Mrs Timms,' she offered.

And so the four of them went to meet William.

'Oh Martha!' he said, when he saw them. 'Why did you bring the little ones? We'll have to be careful they don't fall in.'

'She didn't,' said Susie. '*I* said I'd take care of them. Wake up, Martha, are you still asleep or something?'

William looked at Martha, who was walking slowly behind them. 'What's wrong with her?' he whispered.

'I don't know. She's been like that since I went to fetch her.'

'Oh well,' said William, 'she'll probably be all right soon.'

They arrived at the stone bridge. In summer they often swam here, where the river was wider. While Susie sat on the grass playing with the little boys, William walked further along the river to find a good place for fishing, and Martha stood alone on the bridge, staring into the water.

It kept breaking.

William tried fishing with the line that he had brought, but it kept breaking, and it was difficult to mend. 'Susie!' he called. 'Can you come and help me?' He knew that she was better at mending things than he was.

'All right,' Susie called back. 'Now don't go in the water,' she told the boys, as she hurried away to help William.

Martha was standing by the water now, still staring at the river, but not really seeing anything. She felt sleepy and heavy, and she didn't care about anything at all. She looked up when she heard a step on the bridge. A short woman, dressed in old, comfortable-looking clothes, and wearing very large dark glasses, was looking down at her. Martha looked away again.

'Good morning,' said the woman in a deep, soft voice.

'Good morning,' replied Martha dully, kicking a stone into the water.

'I think I've lost my way,' said the woman.

Martha felt too sleepy to answer. But she said unwillingly, 'Were you looking for the Hampden Stones? That's what most people come to look at. They're up the hill there.'

The woman made a little hissing noise. 'Oh, no, that's a bad place, isn't it, dear? We mustn't go there.'

Martha looked stupidly at her. The sun kept catching the woman's glasses and shining in Martha's eyes. She opened her mouth to disagree, and unexpectedly found herself saying something quite different. 'That's right,' she said obediently. 'It's a bad place. We mustn't go there.'

The woman came closer. 'It's time to go, dear. You're coming with me, aren't you, Martha?'

'That's right,' said Martha. 'I'm coming with you.'

The woman held out her hand and Martha took it. They began to walk away over the bridge. The boys stood up and the younger one, Tommy, shouted, 'Martha! Martha! Come back!' But Martha did not turn round.

When Susie and William returned, they were very surprised to hear from the boys that Martha had gone away with a stranger. They looked at each other worriedly.

'Was this stranger a tall lady with black hair and a kind of white face? Wearing a fur coat?' asked Susie.

'No, she had big black glasses on!' said Tommy.

'Oh,' said Susie, relieved. 'Just for a moment I thought

. . . Still, Martha shouldn't go off with a stranger like that.'

'We'd better go after her and find her,' said William.

They began to hurry along, with the two boys running behind them, but did not manage to catch up with the woman and Martha until they reached the road. They were just in time to see Martha and the woman getting into the big black Rolls Royce. Martha did not look round when Susie screamed at her, but the woman did. The car drove quickly away.

All the way back to the village Susie was talking angrily. 'Why did she do it? How stupid she is! What'll we do, William? Oh, I'll have something to say to her when we find her . . .'

'Don't go on like that, Susie,' said William. 'We'll find her. It'll be all right.'

They pushed the boys in through the Timms' back door, and went straight to find Miss Hepplewhite.

'You say Martha seemed strange today?' she asked, when Susie had told her the whole story. 'Yes, I am afraid that woman was Morgan – she takes many different shapes, you know – and she has got hold of Martha. We must get the poor girl back at once. This time we have to move on to Morgan's ground. Are you prepared to do that?'

'We certainly are,' said William. 'Poor old Martha . . . But where do you think Morgan has taken her?'

'I know,' Susie said suddenly. 'Mr Steel's got that big house just outside Chipping Ledbury. She could be there.'

'Very likely,' said Miss Hepplewhite. 'Very likely. Large.

Fortunately a lorry stopped.

Private. Yes, I think that is where you will find Martha . . .'

There was no bus to Chipping Ledbury for an hour and a half, so Susie and William waited on the road leading out of the village. Fortunately a lorry soon stopped, and the driver offered to take them. During the journey the children sat on the edge of their seats, worrying about what was happening to Martha.

Twenty minutes later the lorry was moving slowly through the lunch-time traffic in Chipping Ledbury, then at last they were out of the town and driving through the countryside.

'Here,' said Susie, when she saw a high wall and big black gates. 'Can we get out here, please?' They got down from the lorry, which drove off, leaving them alone on the empty road.

Walking through the open gates, they could see the chimneys and roof of a big house, surrounded by trees and large gardens. They began to walk towards the house, moving from tree to tree, and staying hidden as much as possible. Just then the front of the house came into view.

It was very large and very grand, with rows of windows, and wide stone steps leading up to the double front doors. Everything was very quiet.

Susie gasped. There, right in front of the house, was the Rolls, sleeping in the sun like a fat black cat.

7
Finding Martha

'She must be here,' whispered Susie. 'Now what'll we do?' The house was so large and important-looking! She was afraid, not only of Morgan, but also of the owners, who could appear at any moment, and ask what they were doing.

William was thinking hard. 'Morgan's probably hidden her somewhere. We'll have to look for her. You aren't frightened, are you?'

'Oh no,' said Susie quickly.

'I know,' suggested William. 'Let's try and find the man who was driving the Rolls the other day, Mr Steel's driver. Perhaps he'll tell us where Martha is.'

'All right,' said Susie. 'Look, that must be him, round the side of the house, where the garages are. Go on, you ask him.'

William hesitated. His hands felt hot and wet, and his heart was beating loudly. The man, who was sitting outside the garage, reading a newspaper, looked perfectly normal, but you never knew. William breathed deeply a few times, and walked bravely out into the sunshine. The man looked up. 'Yes?' he said coldly. 'What do you want?'

'It's about the Rolls,' said William. 'The girl who got into it this morning – she's a friend of ours. There's been a mistake – she didn't really want to come here. We've got to take her home. Please – do you know where she is?'

The man stared at William. 'I don't know what you're talking about,' he said. 'There isn't any girl here, as far as I know. The Rolls hasn't been out today.'

'Yes, it has!' said William desperately. 'We saw it, in Steeple Hampden. Perhaps she – Mrs Steel – was driving it.'

'What do you want?'

48

'She can't drive,' said the man. 'I always drive the Rolls. And I'm telling you, it hasn't been out today. Now go away, or there'll be trouble. She's told me to make sure there are no strangers around, and she gets angry if anyone disobeys her.'

William moved backwards, his heart beating uncomfortably. 'Sorry, I'll go now.' He ran back to where Susie was hiding and told her what the man had said. 'He wasn't telling lies,' he added. 'I just don't understand about the car.'

The sun was no longer shining, and a cool wind was blowing around them. 'You know,' said Susie. 'I don't like it here. I'm frightened, and that's a fact.'

'Oh,' said William, relieved, 'are you? So am I. But we've got to go on. We've got to find Martha.'

'The only thing we can do is to look for her in the house.'

They walked quietly round to the back of the house, where they found an open door and went in. They were in a large, dark room, full of heavy, uncomfortable-looking furniture. They could hear voices in the kitchen, but they did not meet anybody. Taking their shoes off, they walked straight through to the hall, and then up the wide stairs. The stone floor was icy under their feet, and they felt terribly afraid. If one of the doors opened now . . . But nothing happened.

One by one they opened the doors on the first floor. Bathrooms, bedrooms, cupboards . . . And then they found themselves in a larger bedroom, where a woman's dress lay on a chair. Through the open windows they could see the garden, and someone on a white horse riding up to the front door. Susie suddenly felt very cold, and she looked at William. 'Yes,' he whispered, 'I can feel her too.'

And then Susie saw it, lying on the carpet in a corner. A sweet paper, red and white, the kind that her mother sold in the village shop. Together she and William ran to the door on the other side of the room, and pushed it open. They were looking into another, much smaller room.

Martha was sitting there, in the middle of the room, staring at the wall, with a half-full packet of sweets beside her.

'Oh, Martha, we were so worried about you!' said William 'I'm so glad we've found you! Are you all right?'

Susie felt very relieved. Crossly she said, 'We've been looking everywhere for you. You are *stupid*, Martha – the door wasn't locked – why didn't you just walk out?'

Martha looked at them with polite interest, but said nothing.

'Martha!' said William. 'What's the matter? Don't you know who we are?'

'Yes,' said Martha dully. 'You're William. She's Susie.'

Susie took Martha's arm. 'Come on, Martha! Morgan'll be back any minute.'

'That's right,' said Martha calmly. 'She'll be back soon.'

'Help me, William,' said Susie angrily. 'We'll have to make her come with us.' Between them they pulled Martha to her feet and back into the larger room. They had almost reached the door when they heard footsteps on the stairs. William hesitated but Susie said, 'There's no other way out. We've got to get down the stairs!' Holding Martha's hands, they opened the door and ran out.

Morgan was waiting for them on the stairs. She was wearing a black jacket and high, shiny riding boots. Her face was white and frightening, her eyes dark and terrible.

But before she had time to turn and catch them, William and Susie, pulling Martha between them, had reached the bottom of the stairs and were running out of the open front door into the bright air.

They hurried through the gardens towards the road, running from tree to tree, and avoiding any open ground. For five minutes they ran without speaking or looking behind them. 'We'd better not stop,' gasped Susie. 'We must just get to Chipping. We'll be all right where there are lots of people.'

They ran on, with Susie still pulling Martha by the hand. Now there was a distant beating sound, and the ground seemed to tremble. The noise was getting louder, and Susie could not stop herself looking over her shoulder. Behind them, coming closer and closer, was a dark figure on a large white horse. It was chasing them! They could hear the animal breathing hard, as they ran the last two hundred metres through the trees. Only Martha seemed reluctant to get away, and Susie had to push and pull her. They climbed over the wall, and dropped down on to the road.

There was a bus at the bus stop, and they jumped on

just as it was beginning to move away. White and exhausted, they threw themselves into a seat. William paid for their tickets with some coins he had in his pocket. 'But this bus only goes to Chipping,' he whispered to Susie. 'We'll have to go to the bus station and wait for a bus to the village.' He looked worriedly at Martha. 'She's still under Morgan's spell, isn't she?'

'Perhaps she'll be all right if we keep her away from Morgan.'

The bus had reached the town. They got off, and began to walk through the busy streets towards the bus station. The town was crowded with people doing their shopping. Nobody looked at them. They were just three children in a hurry. 'How could we ever explain to anybody what's really happening to us?' thought William. 'We're fighting a deadly battle against Morgan – the kind of battle other people have been fighting for hundreds of years. It's like living in a different time. These people just wouldn't understand.'

All the time the sky was growing darker, and rain was beginning to fall. Suddenly William noticed the Rolls parked on the opposite side of the road. It was empty. Morgan was standing near it, wearing a coat and dark glasses, and moving her head from side to side like a snake. At that moment Martha saw her, and made a little sound. Morgan looked straight at them and began to move forwards across the road.

'Quick!' said Susie, and they hurried away, pulling

52

Martha along with them.

'Where shall we go?' said William desperately. 'She'll trap us if we aren't careful.'

Suddenly Susie said, 'The church! Miss Hepplewhite said Morgan hates the sign of the cross. And churches always have a back door.'

They hurried on, hoping that Morgan would not see where they were going, and finally reached the church. William opened the big, heavy wooden door, and they stepped into a dark coolness, smelling of stone and flowers.

8
Escaping from Morgan

The church was empty. 'Oh dear!' said Susie. 'There's nobody here! Nobody to help us if Morgan comes.'

'It doesn't matter,' said William. 'It's just her against us, anyway, isn't it? Nobody *can* help us.'

They were walking through the church towards the large stone cross high up on the wall, when suddenly they heard the door open behind them. At once they dropped down behind one of the large wooden seats, and waited. The door closed again, and then the church was silent.

At last William put his head over the top of the seat. He saw Morgan standing by the door, her snake-eyes looking in all the dark corners of the building. She looked uncomfortable, like a cat stepping into water. Susie and

William both felt very cold, and their bodies were trembling. Martha did not seem to feel anything. She moved her arm, and a pile of books fell on the floor with a crash. The noise seemed very loud, and Susie and William froze. Now they could hear the sound of Morgan's footsteps coming towards them. Suddenly the whole building rang with noise. The clock was striking, and the echo of the bells sounded from floor to roof and from wall to wall.

Pulling Martha with them, William and Susie ran across the church, and hid behind a round stone column. The church was silent again, but the dark figure in the shadows was moving towards them. When a deathly cold entered their bones, they knew that Morgan was very near. They ran towards the door, and hid behind another column. They heard Morgan laughing. A low voice said, 'Martha, come here.'

'Sorry,' Martha said to William and Susie, 'I'm afraid I've got to go now.' She shook Susie's hand from her arm, stepped away from the column and walked towards Morgan.

'Stop, Martha!' cried Susie. But Martha did not seem to hear, and went on walking. Desperately, the others ran after her. Morgan was waiting for Martha near the door, her face white and expressionless. But suddenly she stepped back in horror. She had noticed a cross on the stone floor by her feet.

She hates the sign of the cross . . .

Morgan hissed like a snake, and fell back.

Susie looked round wildly. The big silver church crosses were too heavy for her to lift, but there was a small cross made of straw on a column beside the door. She took it quickly and ran up to Morgan, holding it out in front of her.

Morgan hissed like a snake, and fell back. And then she screamed, and the sound filled the church for several seconds. Then it was gone, and so was Morgan. The children were standing alone, staring at the place where she had been.

Susie put the cross back on the column, and together they all moved out into the everyday world of the street.

'We'll have to do something about Martha,' Susie said. 'Let's take her to the hospital. Perhaps they can help her.

55

Anyway, it's a good place to hide from Morgan.'

They went to Chipping Ledbury Hospital, where they did not have to wait long for the doctor to look at Martha. He had very dark skin, a thin bony face, and intelligent brown eyes. 'Probably Indian or something,' thought William. The doctor listened to Martha's chest, shone a bright light into her eyes, and turned her head from side to side. She lay on the bed, staring up at him, and answered his questions politely, while the others sat beside her, looking worried.

'Well,' he said in the end, 'if we were in my country, I'd say she was under some evil person's spell. I have seen this kind of thing before. Fortunately she is beginning to get better. Give her a cup of tea, would you, nurse? Then she can go home.'

'Really!' said the nurse, when she brought the tea. 'These foreign doctors! Who believes in spells these days!' And she hurried out, shaking her head. By now Martha was sitting up and looking almost normal. 'Where am I?' she asked.

'In the hospital,' replied Susie. 'You've been behaving very strangely. We think Morgan put a spell on you. Don't you remember? You went off in the car with her.'

Martha's mouth dropped open. 'Did I? I don't remember that. But I *do* remember last night. I woke up and looked out of the window. There was a strong wind, and – I saw the Stones.'

'The Stones?' repeated William. 'How could you?

56

You can't see them from your house.'

'That's just it,' replied Martha. 'They were moving.'

The others stared at her. 'Moving?' said William.

'And there was something else,' said Martha. 'But I can't remember what it was.'

'Never mind,' said Susie, getting up. 'Let's try and get to the bus station before Morgan finds us again.'

Just then the nurse came back into the room. 'Ah!' she said brightly. 'You're very lucky. A kind lady has offered to take you all home in her lovely big car. Come along now.'

'We aren't allowed to go with strangers,' said Susie.

'But this is all right, dear, I promise you, because this lady isn't a stranger. She's Mr Steel's wife. We all know him.'

'Well, we're not going with her,' said Martha. By now they were all walking towards the big double doors, and they could see a dark figure standing by the entrance. William suddenly shouted, 'Run!' and they had gone through the doors and were outside before anyone could stop them. They kept on running towards the bus station, without looking behind them. It was raining hard now. There was no sound of following footsteps.

They were relieved to see that the Steeple Hampden bus was waiting with its engine running. Gasping for breath, they climbed in and sat down right at the back. They stared worriedly out of the windows, hoping the bus would start soon. There were several people they knew on the bus, but no sign of Morgan. In a few minutes the driver appeared, the doors closed, and the bus started moving slowly away.

Outside, the rain was beating on the windows, and the sky was dark. But inside, it felt pleasantly warm and safe, and the children began to feel much better.

Suddenly Martha gave a cry, and the others turned. Behind the bus was a large, shiny black car. It was the Rolls.

'Look!' said William in a shaken voice. 'There isn't anyone driving it.'

'There isn't anyone driving it.'

58

It was perfectly true. The Rolls slid silently behind the bus, but there was nobody at the wheel. In the back they could just see a pair of long legs, crossed.

'It can't be . . .' said William, but the girls said nothing. Clearly it could be, and, in fact, must be – Morgan.

'That explains why the driver said the Rolls hadn't been out,' whispered Susie.

One of their neighbours from Steeple Hampden was sitting in front of William. He bent forward and said politely to her, 'Excuse me, but do you see that car behind the bus?'

'Yes, my dear, a grand-looking car,' the woman replied.

'Can you see anything strange about it?' he asked.

'No, my dear, nothing strange,' the woman answered, a little impatiently. 'But I don't know much about cars.'

The children looked at each other, and remembered Miss Hepplewhite's words.

Most people only see what they expect to see . . .

9
Morgan and the Stones

The bus was coming into Steeple Hampden now. They passed the barn, and Miss Hepplewhite's house. Susie said, 'We should go and tell her that Martha's all right.'

'How can we?' said William. 'Morgan's still following us.'

'What's she *doing*?' asked Susie worriedly.

'She's chasing us, that's what she's doing. Before, *we* were looking for *her*, to find Martha. Now *she* wants to find *us*.'

The bus stopped outside the pub, and the children got off reluctantly, keeping close to people they knew. But the other passengers hurried away to their homes, and soon the street was empty except for the children and the black Rolls.

'Come on,' said Susie. 'We've got to get away from her. It's no good going home. She can find us there.' They walked down the street, looking unhappily over their shoulders from time to time. The Rolls was following them. They started running, but the big car just went faster. When they reached the last house in the village, they ran up to the door and knocked wildly. Old Mrs Tomkins opened the door.

'Please can we come in?' cried Susie wildly. 'That car is following us – please let us in!'

'What car?' said Mrs Tomkins, looking out, 'that one? But it's just standing there! If you're playing games with me, Susie, I don't think it's at all funny. And I'll tell your mother if you do it again! Now run along home, all of you!' The door closed.

'I said it was just us against her,' said William. 'Nobody else is involved.' His face was very white.

'Let's go into the fields,' Susie suggested. 'Then she'll have to chase us on foot, without the car.'

They climbed a gate into the nearest field. It was full of tall, golden corn, all the way from the road to the river.

'If we go down to the river,' said William, 'we can hide in the bushes there, and then if she doesn't find us, and goes away, we can make a circle back to the village.'

'All right,' agreed Susie. 'We've got to do something.'

They stared running across the cornfield. After a minute they stopped and looked back. 'Oh no!' cried William in horror. The Rolls had simply crashed through the gate and was driving right across the field towards them.

The children went on running, but it was difficult to run fast through the wet corn. They were moving slowly and heavily, like swimmers, and all the time the car was coming closer. As the Rolls banged over the rough ground, birds flew up in surprise, and there was a line of damaged corn behind it.

'Nearly there . . .' gasped William. 'Jump over the bushes . . . down to the water.'

'I can't go in the water!' cried Martha. 'I can't swim!'

But William shouted over his shoulder. 'It's all right! I know a hiding-place there! It's safe! Jump, Martha, jump!'

She jumped, shutting her eyes, and hearing Susie beside her. They slid down through the bushes towards the water's edge, but suddenly found themselves on a wide rock just above the river.

'Get back!' said William, and they all pushed themselves to the back of the rock, under the thick bushes that grew out from the steep river bank above them. There was a

They saw the car crashing through the bushes.

terrible noise over their heads, and then they saw the black shape of the car crashing through the bushes and on down into the river. The water rose high around it and the ground shook. And as this happened, the rainstorm moving across the valley reached the Sharnbrook, darkening everything, so that the car's last moments were lost in the driving, beating rain. Thunder crashed across the sky, and there was lightning on the car roof.

Or was it lightning? Holding each other's trembling hands, they saw it, but afterwards they were not sure.

There was light, and a hissing sound, and a kind of electricity in the air. And then the car was gone, and they heard thunder again.

But there was another noise that was not thunder. It seemed to come from the air, just above the car's resting-place. A thin, high crying, which became a scream, and then lost itself in the rain. It was an ugly, evil, crazy sound. When Martha heard it, she cried, 'Don't listen! That's what I heard in the night! We mustn't listen!' The scream rose again over the river, but the children kept their fingers in their ears, their hearts beating wildly. Then, carefully, William took his hands away. The noise had gone. The thunder was more distant, and the rain was falling less heavily. 'It's all right, it's gone,' he said to the girls. 'But Morgan hasn't gone far away. I can still feel her.'

'That noise was awful!' said Martha. 'You know, I'm beginning to remember things she said. About the Stones – she said it was a bad place. I think she's afraid of them. And last night, when I looked out of the window and saw them, I thought – they were like an army preparing for battle.'

'I think you're right,' said William. 'You know people call the Stones the Knights, and say they had a battle with an evil queen in the past? Well, I think that was probably Morgan.'

They sat there on the rock, not noticing their wet clothes and cold feet. They thought of the peaceful Hampden Stones, and then of Morgan with her snake head and her inhuman eyes. To all of them came the idea that the Stones and Morgan were the opposite sides of things – good against evil.

'Let's go to the Stones now,' suggested Susie. 'We *must* be safe *there*.'

The others agreed, and they climbed back into the field. There was no sign of Morgan. The birds were silent, just like before a thunderstorm. The children walked beside the river.

It seemed a long way to the Stones. 'We haven't come the wrong way, have we?' William asked. The fields looked different, with long rough grass, and there were far more trees than usual. They could not hear any cars, or planes, or machines anywhere. When they looked back at Steeple Hampden, the roofs of the houses had disappeared, and there was no church. Instead, there were some round shapes on grassy land, with smoke rising from open fires.

'Something's awfully wrong,' said Martha, frightened.

Thunder crashed near them, and it began to rain. Then that terrible scream came down the valley again. Immediately they put their hands over their ears.

'Look!' cried Susie. 'There's a kind of road!' A rough, wide road, cutting through trees and bushes, led straight up the hill.

'It's the old road to the Stones!' cried Martha. The scream came again, right over their heads, then stopped.

They were running up the old road now. Lightning shone somewhere behind the hill. Martha felt very cold, and she could hear a loud, regular, beating noise behind her. She and the others looked round at the same time, and they all saw the same thing. Down in the valley there was a white horse, carrying a dark rider. It was moving fast up the hill behind them, and its heavy feet made the ground under their own feet tremble. They turned and ran as fast as they could, although they were very tired by now, and their breath came in short, painful gasps. To Martha it seemed like the most frightening dream she had ever had. She heard a woman's voice calling her, 'Martha!'

'No!' she shouted back. 'No! I'm not coming with you any more!' But her breathless voice only sounded like a whisper, and nobody seemed to hear.

At last they reached the top of the hill, and there, calm and peaceful, were the Stones. But the two fallen Stones

They ran as fast as they could.

now stood upright, and there was something standing in front of the great central stone inside the circle. Martha gasped. Was it human? Alive? It stepped forward, and they saw it was a woman. She put out a hand to them, calling them to come closer. Lightning shone over the hill for a moment. And in that moment they saw the woman's face.

'Miss Hepplewhite!' said Susie. But she wasn't sure. The face was young and welcoming, but there was also something distant and very old about it, something they had seen before. And then the light went, and so did the figure. The Stones were there, but the circle was empty. And the horse and rider were nearly on top of them.

'Come on!' shouted William. They ran, and as they threw themselves into the circle, they felt the Stones move, making an unbroken wall around the children. Outside, they could hear Morgan's angry scream as the horse's feet beat against the grey wall of stone, but inside, they were safe.

They lay in the long grass, covering their faces with their hands, while all around them the Stones fought their violent battle against Morgan. The air was full of terrible crashes, and thunder, and screams, and bangs, and the ground shook. The battle went on for some time. Once Martha looked between her fingers, and saw grey shapes chasing angrily across the sky, lit by lightning. She realized that it was too awful to watch, and quickly hid her face again. There was a final, evil scream from Morgan, which rose into the air, and then was heard no more. William, his eyes closed, and his ears ringing with noise, thought, 'The Stones have won at last!'

Now the air was silent, the Stones stood calmly looking over the valley again, and the children lay on the ground in peace. Perhaps they slept for a while – they seemed to be there for a long time, longer than the battle had lasted.

They all returned to consciousness at about the same time. One by one they sat up. They could see the road from Chipping Ledbury to Steeple Hampden, with its traffic, and the distant roof of the village church. They could hear the engine of a plane as it flew above their heads. But was it morning or afternoon? It was impossible to tell – the sun was hidden behind the clouds. They felt extremely hungry.

All around them the Stones stood or lay in their usual places, and there was nothing to show that they had ever moved. The children stared at them, wondering.

'I think we'd better go and find Miss Hepplewhite,' said William. They went down the hill, their clothes wet and dirty. There was no longer any sign of the old road through the corn. It had completely disappeared.

10
Back to the village

By the time they reached Miss Hepplewhite's garden, the sun was shining brightly again, and the valley was coming to life after the storm. They knocked at her front door, and when she opened it, she looked hard at them for a moment. Then she said, 'I can see that you have been a long way. But I am very pleased to see you. Come in and have some tea.' They followed her into the kitchen, where there were plates of cakes and bread-and-butter all ready.

Susie asked, almost accusingly, 'Were you expecting us?'

'I was *hoping* to see you, shall we say? Did you get *very* wet during that annoying thunderstorm?'

'Miss Hepplewhite,' said Martha seriously, 'have you been up on the hill today? At the Hampden Stones?'

Miss Hepplewhite's expression did not change, but there was a rather distant look in her eyes. 'The Stones? Ah yes, a very pleasant place. But I'm too old to climb the hill these days. I haven't been there for a long time.'

'*How* long?' asked Martha.

'Not for a very, very long time,' said Miss Hepplewhite, and added quickly, 'No more questions now! Sit down and have some tea.'

The children realized that it must be early afternoon. As they ate, they told her the whole story. When they had finished, she sat back and said with a smile, 'You have done wonderfully well. Your work is over.'

'We didn't really do it alone,' said William. 'The Stones won the battle against her, and sent her away.'

'But you made it possible. You helped them.'

Martha thought, 'We brought Morgan here, with our witch's brew in the barn, but perhaps that was a good thing. Perhaps the Stones were waiting for her. Or Miss Hepplewhite was.' She stared at Miss Hepplewhite's old, lined face, and tried to recognize the strange figure they had seen inside the stone circle. But it was too difficult. She decided not to think about it any more.

Susie was thinking about something else. 'What do you

'*Your work is over.*'

think will happen now about the motorway through the village?'

'I think,' said Miss Hepplewhite, 'that we will very soon hear of a change in the plans. You should not worry about it.'

'Nobody'll ever know that it was us who stopped it,' said William, a little sadly.

'Never mind. *You* will always know. And I shall, too.'

'Will she ever come back?' asked Martha.

'Not in your time, my dear. One day she will. Of course, she lives at different levels of time from you – from us. She is not as strong as she was, and cannot learn anything new now. That is why she goes on using the same spells, and the same weapons.'

A shadow on the wall, a touch of ice, a scream in the

wind, a horse's hot breath . . . Martha remembered, and looked gratefully round the warm, untidy kitchen.

'When was she last here?' asked Susie suddenly.

'Oh, let me see . . . a couple of hundred years ago, if I remember rightly. And of course, she was here in the seventeenth century – I must tell you about that some time. But now I really think you should go home. Your poor parents must be very worried about you!'

They finished their meal, and said goodbye to Miss Hepplewhite. She stood at her front door, a small, bent figure in her long dress and large summer hat, waving to them as they walked away. They realized how much they all liked her.

'Just think,' said William, 'we'll be able to go up to the barn tomorrow, and *play* there, just like before all this began.'

Martha said, 'My Mum'll be angry with me when she sees me. My dress is all dirty!'

'So's mine,' said Susie. 'But I don't care . . . If our parents are angry with us, that's nothing when you think what's happened to us today.'

'What a pity we can't tell anyone about it!' said William. 'They'd laugh at us if we did!'

When they came to the village shop, they noticed people standing in groups, staring towards the river. Suddenly Mrs Poulter, who was talking excitedly to a circle of neighbours, saw the children, and called out angrily, 'You *are* a bad girl, Susie! I've been so worried about you! Where have you been all day? Not back for lunch, and not a word to anyone. And you were out in that terrible storm!'

'Sorry, Mum,' said Susie. 'I really am sorry. But what's everyone looking at?'

Mrs Poulter's eyes shone with interest, and she no longer looked cross. 'There's been a serious accident. You know the big Rolls that belongs to Mr Steel? Someone's driven it right across the field and into the river!'

'Oh dear!' said William, in an unnatural voice. 'Why would anybody do that?'

'Nobody seems to know. The police think it was stolen. They're looking in the river now – for dead bodies.'

'They won't find any,' said Susie calmly.

'What do *you* know about it, miss?' asked her mother.

'Oh, nothing really,' said Susie quickly.

'Just look at your hair! And your dress! Now come straight along with me, young lady, and get changed. And you two had better go home as well!'

The following morning, the people of Steeple Hampden watched with interest as the Rolls was lifted out of the river, and put on a lorry. It was taken away to Chipping Ledbury. No bodies were found in the river. 'I was right, wasn't I?' said Susie, but not loud enough for her mother to hear.

That afternoon, William's father came home waving the local newspaper excitedly. 'Would you believe it! They're going to build that motorway on Mr Steel's land after all! He's going to close down the factory, and sell it!'

William had been expecting this, but he said kindly, 'It must be because of your petition, Dad.'

'Do you really think so? I wonder . . . It would be nice to feel that we had something to do with it.'

'I'm sure you did, Dad. You and the whole village made Mr Steel change his plans. It's fantastic!'

His father smiled happily, as William began to read the newspaper. On the front page, next to a photo of the village, it said:

NEW MOTORWAY

The people of Steeple Hampden will be relieved to hear that the new M10 motorway will probably not go through their village. Last night Mr Steel, owner of the Steel Brothers factory at Chipping Ledbury, said that he was planning to close it down, as he wanted to leave the country immediately. It appears that yesterday afternoon his wife suddenly decided to go abroad, and her husband wishes to join her. It is possible that Mr and Mrs Steel will not return to England. Mr Steel will, therefore, almost certainly agree to sell the factory, and so the new M10 will go south near Chipping Ledbury, across his land. The beautiful village of Steeple Hampden and the Sharnbrook Valley will be safe for our children to enjoy for many more years.

William went out to find Susie and Martha. It was a fine, clear August morning, and the countryside looked clean and shining after the rain. People in the village were busily doing their usual jobs, and everything looked completely normal again. Susie came out of her mother's shop when she saw him, and Martha joined them a few minutes later.

'My Mum's so proud of herself!' said Susie crossly. 'She thinks the village has been saved just because of the petition that everybody signed! Can you believe it!'

'It doesn't really matter,' said Martha. 'Not really.'

'Well, I could tell her who *really* saved the village from the motorway.'

'You mustn't,' said William.

'I know,' said Susie, more calmly. 'I suppose it isn't so bad, knowing something that nobody else knows. It makes you feel good, doesn't it?'

'Shall we go to the barn?' suggested William.

'Not yet,' said Martha. 'First let's go . . .'

'I know. To the Stones.'

'Yes,' said Susie. 'That's what I was thinking too. Just to see they're all right. It would show how' – she searched for the right words – 'how grateful we are.'

They began to climb the hill. Cloud shadows moved across the corn in front of them, and between the shadows ran the faint line of an old road.

GLOSSARY

barn a large farm building for keeping hay or corn in

corn plants growing in a field, cereals like wheat or maize

evil very bad

faint describing something that you cannot see clearly

foam a thick white mass of very small air bubbles in a liquid

gasp to take in quick deep breaths because of fear, surprise, or because you need more air

god a being who is believed to have power over us

hiss to make a long 's' sound; snakes make this sound

interviewer someone whose job is asking questions on television or radio

knight (in the past) a noble soldier on a horse, who fought against evil people or things

motorway a wide modern road where traffic can travel fast

petition a special letter signed by many people, asking for or protesting about something

relieved glad that a problem has gone away

reluctant unwilling to do something

science the study of natural things; physics, chemistry, etc. are sciences

spell words which when spoken are thought to have magical power

strike (past tense **struck**) (of a clock) to tell the time by sounding a bell

suggest to offer ideas or say what you think someone should do

unpleasant not nice, not enjoyable

weakness not being strong

witch a woman who uses magic to do evil things

The Whispering Knights

ACTIVITIES

Before Reading

1 The title of the story is *The Whispering Knights*. What do you think the knights are going to be?

   1 people   2 animals   3 stones   4 trees

2 Read the back cover and the story introduction on the first page of the book. Then answer these questions.

   1 What are the names of the three friends in the story?

   2 Which of them is worried about their game?

   3 Who used to live in the old barn?

   4 What is the name of the witch?

3 The friends make a witch's brew. What is a witch? Cross out the words that are wrong.

A witch is usually a *man/woman* who uses *magic/cooking* to do *good/bad* things.

4 What is going to happen in the story? Can you guess? For each sentence, circle Y (Yes) or N (No).

   1 Morgan le Fay will come back. Y/N

   2 The children will fight Morgan. Y/N

   3 Miss Hepplewhite will die. Y/N

   4 The Whispering Knights will help the children. Y/N

While Reading

Read Chapters 1 and 2. Who said this, and who or what were they talking about?

1 'It's what witches used to do!'
2 'Does it matter? Have we done anything wrong?'
3 '. . . she's the bad side of things, you see.'
4 '. . . it talks to itself.'
5 'I remember her when I was a boy.'
6 'It was just a bad dream, that's all.'
7 'Look at its head!'
8 'I must say, I don't think much of her first attempt.'

Before you read Chapter 3, can you guess the answers to these questions? The title of the chapter is: *A cake for Susie*.

1 What sort of cake will it be?
2 Who will give it to her?
3 Will she eat it?

Now read Chapter 3. Are these sentences true (T) or false (F)? Rewrite the false sentences with the correct information.

1 Susie's mother had a shop.
2 There was a problem with all the televisions in the village.
3 The big new road was not going to go through the village.

Read Chapter 4. Are these sentences true (T) or false (F)? Rewrite the false sentences with the correct information.

1 Morgan was afraid of the sign of the cross.
2 The Hampden Stones were not very old.
3 Martha was frightened of the Stones.
4 The Stones moved around all the time.
5 The line across the field was an old road to the Stones.
6 The woman in the Rolls Royce was Morgan le Fay.

Read Chapters 5 and 6 and answer these questions.

Why

1 . . . did Miss Hepplewhite want the children to help with the petition?
2 . . . was Mr Steel behaving strangely when he appeared on television?
3 . . . did William shout?
4 . . . did the stone column disappear?
5 . . . did Martha wake up in the night?
6 . . . did Susie leave the little boys by the river?
7 . . . did William and Susie go in the lorry?
8 . . . did William and Susie go to Mr Steel's house?

Read Chapters 7 and 8. Choose the best question-word for these questions, and then answer them.

Who / What / How

1 . . . did William and Susie ask about Martha?

2 . . . was riding a white horse?

3 . . . did the children escape from Morgan?

4 . . . did Susie use to make Morgan go away?

5 . . . did the doctor say was wrong with Martha?

6 . . . offered to take the children home in her car?

7 . . . was driving the car that was following the bus?

Read Chapters 9 and 10. Match these halves of sentences and use the linking words to make a paragraph of seven sentences. (You will need to use some linking words more than once.)

and then / but / because / in the end / so / so that / when

1 the children ran through the field _____

2 _____ the car followed them across the field _____

3 _____ the children decided to go to the Stones _____

4 _____ they got there and threw themselves into the circle

5 the Stones fought a battle with Morgan _____

6 people found the car in the river _____

7 _____ the motorway was not going to be built through the village _____

8 they thought they would be safe there.

9 there were no dead bodies.

10 crashed into the river.

11 the Stones moved to make a wall to protect them.

12 Morgan would have to chase them on foot.

13 Mr Steel decided to close his factory and go abroad.

14 they returned to their usual places.

After Reading

1 Complete this chart about Morgan le Fay. Then use the information to write a short description of her.

other name	
hair	
skin	
eyes	
rides	
drives in	
hates	
doesn't understand	

2 What were the five things that Morgan le Fay did to frighten the children in Chapters 2–5? Write them next to their names.

Martha _____

Susie _____

William _____

all three children _____ _____

3 Write down everything from the story that suggests there was some mystery about Miss Hepplewhite. Why did she know so much about Morgan? Who do you think she really was?

4 **Imagine that you are Martha. Complete her diary for the day when the children made the witch's brew in the barn.**

Tuesday

Today I went to _____ barn with William and _____. We made a fire _____ cooked a witch's brew. _____ had frogs' legs in _____ and I felt very _____ for the frogs. It _____ William's idea; he had _____ about it in an _____ book. I was worried _____ I thought perhaps it _____ be dangerous, but William _____ afraid because he doesn't _____ in superstitions. Then old _____ Hepplewhite arrived and told _____ that we had done _____ dangerous, because a witch _____ Morgan le Fay had _____ in the barn a _____ time ago. Miss Hepplewhite _____ us to be very _____. It was horrible – I _____ as cold as ice, _____ William and Susie were _____ too, though they said _____ was because of the _____. I'm sure something terrible _____ going to happen!

Now imagine that you are William and write his diary for the same day.

81

5 Imagine that you live in Steeple Hampden and you want to write a letter to the Chipping Ledbury newspaper about the motorway. Complete the letter. You can use as many words as you want.

Dear Sir

The people of Steeple Hampden are very worried because
_____. This road will destroy _____. Steeple
Hampden is _____. We do not want _____. We
believe that it would be better _____. We think Mr
Steel _____.

Yours faithfully

_____

6 Imagine that Susie tried to tell her mother what really happened at the Stones. Complete the conversation. You can use as many words as you want.

SUSIE: You think your petition saved the village but it was
    really _____. They fought _____.
SUSIE'S MUM: Don't be silly, dear! Who's Morgan le Fay?
SUSIE: She's _____.
SUSIE'S MUM: You know there are no such things as witches.
    And the Stones can't move!
SUSIE: But they did! They made _____. And we heard
    _____ and saw _____.
SUSIE'S MUM: That was the thunderstorm, dear.

7 Complete the table with words from the story. Then use some
  of the adjectives to compare:

  Susie/Martha; Martha/William; Morgan/the Stones
  For example: *Susie was more confident than Martha.*

noun	adjective	opposite adjective
danger	_____	_____
_____	noisy	_____
_____	confident/brave	frightened
stupidity	_____	_____
_____	dark	_____
beauty	_____	_____
warmth	_____	_____
goodness	_____	_____
_____	weak	_____

8 'But witches with tall hats and black cats and so on, that's just
  superstition.' Which British superstitions do you know? Use
  the table below to write five sentences about superstitions. Are
  they the same in your country? Add five more from your
  country. Do you believe in them?

	walk underneath	black cat	
lucky unlucky	open see break look at	mirror ladder new moon umbrella	in a house through glass walk across your path

ABOUT THE AUTHOR

Penelope Lively was born in Egypt in 1933; you can read about her childhood in her book *Oleander, Jacaranda*. She went to school in England and then went to Oxford University, where she met her husband, a university teacher. She began to write when her children were growing up and has written a large number of very popular books for children and adults. Perhaps the most famous of her children's books is *The Ghost of Thomas Kempe*, which in 1973 won the Carnegie Medal (a prize for the best children's book of the year).

The Whispering Knights, which was written in 1971, was suggested by the Rollright Stones, a mysterious group of very old stones in a field, which you can visit in North Oxfordshire. Many of Penelope Lively's books are about the way that the past and the present are joined together. She believes that children need to feel that we live in a world that reaches far behind and ahead of us, and that they themselves will change and develop.

ABOUT BOOKWORMS

OXFORD BOOKWORMS LIBRARY
Classics • True Stories • Fantasy & Horror • Human Interest
Crime & Mystery • Thriller & Adventure

The OXFORD BOOKWORMS LIBRARY offers a wide range of original and adapted stories, both classic and modern, which take learners from elementary to advanced level through six carefully graded language stages:

Stage 1 (400 headwords)   Stage 4 (1400 headwords)
Stage 2 (700 headwords)   Stage 5 (1800 headwords)
Stage 3 (1000 headwords)   Stage 6 (2500 headwords)

More than fifty titles are also available on cassette, and there are many titles at Stages 1 to 4 which are specially recommended for younger learners. In addition to the introductions and activities in each Bookworm, resource material includes photocopiable test worksheets and Teacher's' Handbooks, which contain advice on running a class library and using cassettes, and the answers for the activities in the books.

Several other series are linked to the OXFORD BOOKWORMS LIBRARY. They range from highly illustrated readers for young learners, to playscripts, non-fiction readers, and unsimplified texts for advanced learners.

Oxford Bookworms Starters   *Oxford Bookworms Factfiles*
Oxford Bookworms Playscripts   *Oxford Bookworms Collection*

Details of these series and a full list of all titles in the OXFORD BOOKWORMS LIBRARY can be found in the *Oxford English* catalogues. A selection of titles from the OXFORD BOOKWORMS LIBRARY can be found on the next pages.

We Didn't Mean to Go to Sea

ARTHUR RANSOME

Retold by Ralph Mowat

The four Walker children never meant to go to sea. They had promised their mother they would stay safely in the harbour, and would be home on Friday in time for tea.

But there they are in someone else's boat, drifting out to sea in a thick fog. When the fog lifts, they can turn round and sail back to the harbour. But then comes the wind and the storm, driving them out even further across the cold North Sea . . .

The Silver Sword

IAN SERRAILLIER

Retold by John Escott

Jan opened his wooden box and took out the silver sword. 'This will bring me luck,' he said to Mr Balicki. 'And it will bring you luck because you gave it to me.'

The silver sword is only a paper knife, but it gives Jan and his friends hope. Hungry, cold, and afraid, the four children try to stay alive among the ruins of bombed cities in war-torn Europe. Soon they will begin the long and dangerous journey south, from Poland to Switzerland, where they hope to find their parents again.

The Eagle of the Ninth

ROSEMARY SUTCLIFF

Retold by John Escott

In the second century AD, when the Ninth Roman Legion marched into the mists of northern Britain, not one man came back. Four thousand men disappeared, and the Eagle, the symbol of the Legion's honour, was lost.

Years later there is a story that the Eagle has been seen again. So Marcus Aquila, whose father disappeared with the Ninth, travels north, to find the Eagle and bring it back, and to learn how his father died. But the tribes of the north are wild and dangerous, and they hate the Romans . . .

Treasure Island

ROBERT LOUIS STEVENSON

Retold by John Escott

'Suddenly, there was a high voice screaming in the darkness: "Pieces of eight! Pieces of eight! Pieces of eight!" It was Long John Silver's parrot, Captain Flint! I turned to run . . .'

But young Jim Hawkins does not escape from the pirates this time. Will he and his friends find the treasure before the pirates do? Will they escape from the island, and sail back to England with a ship full of gold?

Lorna Doone

R. D. BLACKMORE

Retold by David Penn

One winter's day in 1673 young John Ridd is riding home from school, across the wild lonely hills of Exmoor. He has to pass Doone valley – a dangerous place, as the Doones are famous robbers and murderers. All Exmoor lives in fear of the Doones.

At home there is sad news waiting for young John, and he learns that he has good reason to hate the Doones. But in the years to come he meets Lorna Doone, with her lovely smile and big dark eyes. And soon he is deeply, hopelessly, in love . . .

This Rough Magic

MARY STEWART

Retold by Diane Mowat

The Greek island of Corfu lies like a jewel, green and gold, in the Ionian sea, where dolphins swim in the sparkling blue water. What better place for an out-of-work actress to relax for a few weeks?

But the island is full of danger and mysteries, and Lucy Waring's holiday is far from peaceful. She meets a rude young man, who seems to have something to hide. Then there is a death by drowning, and then another . . .